Beautiful Princess

By R.J.

Copyright @2021 by R.J.

All rights reserved. No part of this publication may be reproduced, stored in a retrieval system, or transmitted in any form or by any means electronic, mechanical, photocopying, recording, or otherwise without the written permission of the authors.

Limits of Liability-Disclaimer

The authors and publisher shall not be liable for your misuse of this material. The purpose of this book is to educate and empower. The authors and/or publisher do not guarantee that anyone following these techniques, suggestions, tips, ideas, and/or strategies will become successful.

The authors and/or publisher shall have neither liability nor responsibility to anyone with respect to any loss or damage caused or alleged to be caused directly or indirectly by the information contained in this book.

ISBN: 978-1-7363669-3-6

Published By: InspiredByVanessa

www.InspiredByVanessa.com

Dedication

Dear Daughter,

You are the light of my eye, the greatest gift, the smaller me. You hold so many great things. Your future is bright. You have the world as your playground, and you can do and be who you want. You are a shining star on the road to success. You will strive and grow into a powerful queen making moves, leaving legacies.

Sincerely,

Mom

I am beautiful, but I am brave.

I am a beautiful princess, but
I will be a beauty queen one day.

I believe in myself. I can do anything I want to do. The world is my oyster; the sky is the limit.

I am a beautiful princess, and
I will be a beauty queen one day.

I am beautiful. I am a superhero. I have superpowers. Call me Wonder Woman because I make things happen.

I am strong, and I am proud. A beautiful princess getting ready to be a beauty queen.

I am beautiful. I am magical. My superpower is to be excellent. I will be respected, and I will leave a name.

I am a beautiful princess, and I will be a beauty queen one day. I will continue to walk tall and stand up for others like me because I believe in girl power—it is imperative.

I am a beautiful princess.
My superpower is super strengthened because I am a strong woman getting ready to sit on my throne.

I am a princess, but I am invincible.
I am a believer and a big dreamer.

I am a beautiful princess, and I will be a beauty queen one day. My mind speaks volumes. My soul is loud.

My outcomes will be
even more influential.

I have a path, and my momma started it for me, but it's up to me to become complete.

I am a beautiful princess, and I will be a beauty queen one day. I believe in other princesses like me fixing upcoming queens' crowns.

I am a princess growing to be something greater. I am a princess becoming whatever I want to be.

There is no limit to what I can become. I have no competition because it is not a race. I am a princess. I twirl and dance.

I am a princess with poise and grace. I am a princess with a determined attitude. I am a princess setting a foundation for my future endeavors.

I look up to queens now that started off as princesses like me. I look up to Michelle Obama, Serena and Venus Williams, Kamala Harris, Maya Angelou, and Ruth Bader Ginsburg. I have so much aspiration to look up to.

I am a princess destined for magnitude. I will be a queen one day, and I will wear my crown proudly. This is my time to speak volumes and excellence to all girls around the world. We can do anything, and we set the pace of the world. We run the world.

I leave by saying this: I am a princess, and I cannot wait to be a queen one day. I will rule the world and make a way for all other girls coming up in the world.

I will be that woman to rule the world, the next president. I am speaking my outcomes into existence. Women rule the world.

About the Authors

Jade R Bryant-Moore was born and raised on the southside of Chicago. She's oldest of five siblings, raised by my grandmother from a young age and instilled I was destined for greatness. Jade excelling elementary with academic honors and graduating top ten in my senior class from Chicago International Charter School Longwood Campus. She knew at that moment she was at the top to have a minor setback in college but finally finished in July 2020 with her Bachelor's in Correctional Support Services with two honor societies under my belt with a GPA of 3.4. She then decided to attack her Masters in Clinical Mental Health Counseling also being a mother of five beautiful kids excelling in motherhood.

Jade is also a Local School Council Chairwoman at Brennemann Elementary and Outreach Coordinator in Parent Advisory Council. She is a force to be reckon with and making changes by bringing awareness to her community and being a part of so many elite outreach organizations.

Jade started her own outreach group called Mother's of Women Outreach on Facebook, bringing positive and motivational words to women across the world. Jade is a formidable parent that believes in investing in her children because they hold the future.

This book was meant to convey a message of greatness to young girls. I am a powerhouse, a highly active mom, and I am a firm believer in advocating for our children. Being the Local School Council Chairperson for my children's school Brennemann Elementary and also the Outreach Coordinator for Parent Advisory Council.

Feel free to follow me on Facebook at:

www.FamilyXpressions.com
https://www.facebook.com/jadie.wadie.9
https://www.facebook.com/groups/702779853500218

www.ingramcontent.com/pod-product-compliance
Lightning Source LLC
Chambersburg PA
CBHW060758090426
42736CB00002B/77